When the Stars Begin to Burn

Zaneta Comacho

BookLeaf Publishing

India | USA | UK

Presentation by *BookLeaf Publishing*

Web: www.bookleafpub.com

E-mail: info@bookleafpub.com

ISBN: 9789358319620

First edition 2024

Guyana

Where do the Guyanese get their gear
when there are hardly no shops here?
Hardly a boutique lines the road- made of sand
tracks,

dust in my face.

Each journey, like a trek to any place.
Men stand on the back of pickups,
timbermen to timberlands,
builders to sites,
dust in my eyes.

Flirtation with eyes.
No greetings.

The lush green Amazon sucks life...gives it.

All kinds of beats travel through homes,
front yards, back yards.

Jumping monkeys chained to walls.
Night life, strife.
Who reads here? Jan Carew- more than just a
poet of the year, a countryman telling in prose.

No change given.
See, don't fight for it or you'll fight for your life.

Kids battle for the one chip challenge, some
American accents in the air ruled by patois, no
little England here.

Public roads straddle cul-de-sac towns: Eccles,
Edinburgh, small towns abound.

Everything is a trot away, horses staccato the
way, amid no belt for back-seaters, the Guyanese
way.

Depth

Playing the tango,
that's where I am,
maybe I'd do flamenco or the fandango, have
you heard this poem before?

Lots of Spanish words.
Am I fancy,
think?

Do I need these words to surround me?
Can I be happy in the English sea?
Do I necessarily need to drink tea?

Just playing my cards right
because all I have is my eyesight.

Always

Always be professional or so the text says
How do I do this when I'm always très à l'aise?

Over self-liberalism or laziness you see
Can affect your way of being.

Ganged up, wolfed up
What am I really saying?

Gotta push myself to the limit,
Plain sailing.

What? Overwork, no, lethargy.

Need to rip the imaginary bit off my mouth to
speak the truth.

Avoiding different isms like the plague, gotta get
myself out of this phone booth.

The Parisian Call

You're pulling up to St Pancras where you'll take the Eurostar.

Gone are the days where homelessness in Paris would make you a star.

Tumbleweeding like Ethan Hawk,
Full of gigs and pics,
The Parisian Metro is in fact, the abyss.

Destination Gare du Nord.
Will you stay on the train until it gets to Belgium?

Or will you get off and fight Parisian bedlam?

A haze of Macron and anti-Le Penism,
Will you get your verb agreements in?

Will you fake love at the Arc de Triomphe or the
Tour Eiffel in this city full of sin?

Camus

Blessed are the hearts that can bend
for they can never be broken.
Something that I never heard spoken,
until now.

Albert Camus's words betoken
a slogan,
senses and ideas of France
for the heartless shogun.
Gangsters or pranksters.

Camus, the absurd, is never misspoken.

The Stranger, the Plague and the Fall,
a few works,
not to name them all.

Franco-Algerian, don't we all
want that power of recall.

An exotic life in theatre,
read widely from Paris to Montreal.

Social Media and Me

Tik Tok and I'm not phased,
Shocked my mother,
She thought I was away.

All the rage,
Following people
Dancing with themselves,
You and I.
Can I have a piece of this pie?

Everyone looks so pretty
Starry-eyed and cute.
Lots of tutorials, it's impossible to stay mute.

No hobbies
Is my nose straight enough?
Can I be enough?
Thoughts everytime I scroll,
Foul-mouthed kidults:
Blond, blue, black and gold.

Michael didn't last to see this jack,
Will I ever get a foothold on this digital map?

Menace to the devil or else I'm procrastinating
another year.

Thoughts resound.
My Bible digitised, too easy to read now.
Will I give it up?

Waiting for change to come and it doesn't
through rational action.
New make-up I've bought
to add some attraction.

Four Am

Four am can I be a sceptic, see
Four am, can you speak Christianese?
Four am, have the pills worn off?

Four am and I'd love someone there,
Four am: only me sees me let down my hair.

Portuguese

Squirrels, cocaine bears n' all,
have my Guyanese family in Canada.

God bless them.

Not a Comacho in sight, this side of GT* land.

I suppose we could try to make amends but
there's no Portuguese people in my ends.

Except a Portuguese lad at my charity who
exchanges looks with a mocha lady, not me.

When the clouds clear I'll see heaven,
I wonder if any of my ancestors will be there.

I don't support Halloween.
Don't want to stay in a lair,

Christ is King, some people have it in ink.

He's a remedy, not a stop-gap chilled drink.

*(Georgetown)

Noticing

Where's the party at in Guyana?
The electricity just came back on.
GT* is in full swing.

Can I be like Jan Carew** and hit you with a
few haiku?

Can I dance in the sand along the side of the
road?

Can I stink from sweating legs, arms, bums and
tums?

Rickety-rick then slide, that's when Rihanna
lights up.

I had an Amerindian guide,
got me out of my blue,
oh how he looks so cool.

Portuguese too,
only, who knew?

*Georgetown
**Guyanese Poet

White Guys Dancing

White guys dancing
to the Brazilian beat
I wasn't born to
To this drum beat.

Raised in a neat and tidy
Notting Hill Gate.
I only saw dancing you could rate
At carnival time, where you could eat
Outside.

The feast of the flesh. Ghouls and ghosts to fear,
Don't let anyone get near.

Lapa in Rio de Janeiro has a marina I didn't see,
But the Copacabana beach, thong out,
With Americans at sea.

The light in Lapa renders black people
luminous,
Shook by the Brazilian beat.

This Lapa is out there,
A bit of a treat.

Long Journey

Making lots of decisions.

Asks her grandma about her heritage.

Grandma calls someone to try and murder her.

She gets a phone call from her ex-best friend.

Her dog bites her grandmother,

Refuses to say what made her split from her grandfather,

So she runs away from her grandmother.

Snap Snap

Snap.

The trees snap under my feet the way MJ
subdued the stage,

The way crocodiles hunt for prey.

I am the king of the jungle in Kingston Upon
Thames just crack squirrels and undercut grass
are under my feet.

I want to be king of the world like Leo in
Titanic. Move down, I want to get a seat.

Gospel

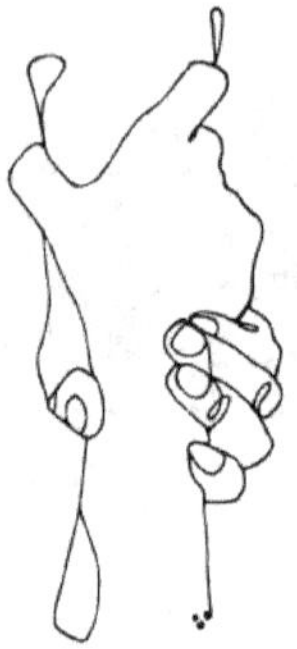

Husky gospel voices,
Will they take me anywhere or will they cause
me despair?

What is freedom of expression versus
Bible-based tale?

Is it a new gospel they're preaching out in
Harlem?

Online threatens our doctrine
Itching ears everywhere,
How can we tell our Luke from our Mark or
revelation from hell?

Jesus is our lighthouse in stormy waters, we
shouldn't be flailing easily.

Our bedrock, the word, guides our tour to a solid
end.

Sin is sin and joy is not just, make that
definition,

Onwards in God we trust.

Activism

"Say their name" they say, for what?

They're trying to make us love the earth to the sky.

Not my mother -the earth - I mean.
I'm not stomping the ground,
I want to ride safely through Cheam.

All our lives matter.
Was George Floyd made an example globally?

All our lives matter, unlike Ye's* tee.

*Ye, short for Kanye West

A Guy On TV

A strange tale to tell.

Too tall to be a model,

Too cute for school.

I saw a guy on TV
Who was made to look like a fool.

In a teddy jacket,
He unveiled his head:
Canerowed or cornrowed- it depends on your
ends.

Comfort Blanket

A lyre played to a king in crisis,
it never denies us.
Like a blanket to a toddler,
it's like the Midas touch.

Glittering in gold in a child's eyes,
it works its charm.
it whispers,
"Never, never, will you be harmed."

Comfort blankets betray us
because they can't sound an alarm,
I would lose a case in the court of law.
of 'baby down' 'tot down',
as they tumble onto the floor.

Coffee

Coffee,
Should I drink it or not?

Please don't take away the pot,
Not "pot" as in ganja.

I don't like the green
But the brown stuff will do.

Putting me on high alert, like kombucha too.
My war on coffee is a war of attrition.

Will I play the game or will I deflect from
addiction?

What You Sow

Some use Bionsen and some use Suave.
I don't use no aluminum.

I don't want any dementia stimulus for no thing,
no not me.

I forgot to tell the organiser that aluminum will
come for you too.

The feel of softness isn't worth the cheap
underarm you just gave me.

What you sow is what you'll reap.

Diary Entry

Defeating the demon of procrastination is my
life's goal.
I want to work past the lethargy,
I want to save my soul.

Quatro Decimans

Easter, what's the history behind this day?
Quatro Decimans,
What's that I hear you say?
Vulgate Latin for the number fourteen,
What Catholics used to call us back in the day,
Who clashed with Christians over the
celebration of Passover,
The fourteenth day of the month Nisan in 325
AD.

Easter was upheld in every area
By the Council of Nicea
Along with the official hysteria
England's Gregorian calendar soon stitched it in.

Among Jews, Pesach is eight days of avoiding
leaven.
Commemorating the Exodus,

Freedom from Egypt
So now we can teach it,
To our children and from the pulpit:
Jesus' rebirth,
No chocolate bunnies, we can own it.

Time to be Human

Like what you like, but not like that.
Rhyme if you want to, attack those who don't.
Don't get stuck in "I won't, I won't."
Not on my hospital bed yet
but I'm not nostalgic about the time,
when nurses and doctors were saying "You're
mine. You're mine."

Fame of immigration
crushing fates at sea.
You are not late to the marathon of "You will be,
you will be."

Dance even if you can't
act with a drama GCSE
be told you are beautiful

be told you are free.

Jump, skip holler,
don't keep a bee in your bonnet, make your
voice heard.

No mountains out of molehills,
be ready on the attack,
level those beasts,
write like a hack.

Unexpected Visitors

Unexpected visitors
expose my shame:
dirty house,
dirty name.

I hide in my home,
like I'm playing a game
with solitude and its friends.

I can't stand the mess,
My family says we can all make amends,
do it yourself, the cleaner can't help

she only does the sharing area.
I'm a little bit keener,
now. That the violent ones are to be evicted

I still feel conflicted
about whether to stay or whether to go.

If the Arab man downstairs invites any more
foes,
cooking up a storm at 4am,
I think it'll turn into bedlam.

The Peace of Wild Things

Dark murky waters where the wood drake rests
Where boats let off their gunk,
Where the fungi grow
Where algae go to meet and greet
Where no one should swim for fear of poisoning
or at worst drowning.

Steady yourself, don't give in.

It's not a Hollywood movie here,
you can't go streaking.

Imagine

Imagine the precipice: don't be afraid, it's
cowardly.

Like Icarus flying too close to the sun,
I am afraid to jump lest I be like he.

Now the stuff of pagan legend.
I do not wish to repeat the same feat, nor
believing in fate.

I will not go down with this ship as it's burning.
I have to find my way out.

Got some clout from my seamen, brothers and
sisters
to jump down and swim, since the Thames is so
grim.

Pleasure is a Thing

The sun's telling me "worship me"
but I tell him I already have a God.

"But I can make you beautiful."
False prophet, I say.

"But, I can lift your mood."
I already drink caffeine, thank you.

"But what about a title?"
I already have a king.

That's Done Now

That's done now,
take it apart, rip its pretty little legs off
take out the stuffing.

Rip off its ugly nose,

No that toy bear isn't for you anymore, we're
reshuffling him, remoulding him.

It's time now.
It's done now.

Your House

Your house,
Splattered with white emulsion,
Apple trees with no smell.

Wooden shed.
Cocoa butter in the mornings.
Pomade.

My house is where the Holy Spirit resides.

How do you feel the pulse of the house is
beating?

Songs: old Pentecostal hymnals.
Smell: of old books.

Your house is your house
Whether your parents are together or not

Say No To Fate

One day you finally knew,
the voices around you kept shouting their bad
advice.

Voices around you kept telling you to
fall over while
you prayed "No way, get out."
Londoners being my vice.

One day you finally knew
that you were sane.

You were never going to pop.
No blood, not even a drop
would come outta you,
no, you had not been royally screwed,
fatality is not yours.

Tell fate to shut itself up.

Destiny is true.

You won't need a rhinoplasty,
surgery is needed for your heart.
You look up without your goggles on as you start.

Past and Present

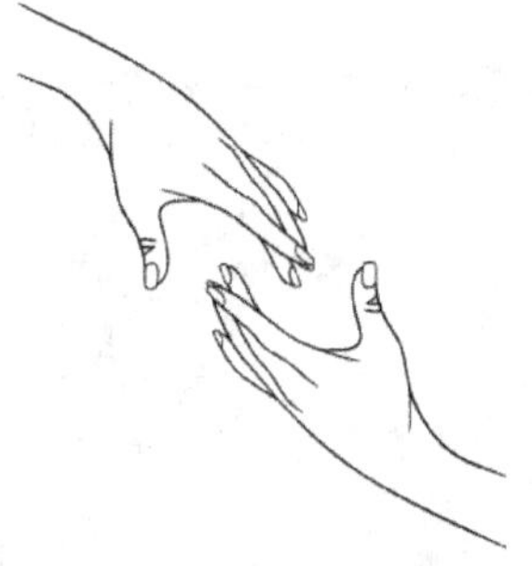

The past is a foreign country,
they do things differently there.

I used to fear that place
but I took a plane to the present,
to live in the moment.

I don't want to be a time traveller.
I want to stay in the gear of 'go' on an
automatic.

No stick shifts for me.

Not like I'm a driver yet or anything,
I'm a being a faith filled futurist.

We believers now.

When the Stars Begin to Burn

Northern lights lure you in,
Manchester, the North, the club, the play,
The university open day.

Stars begin to burn for your future
A prophet's song waiting to be heard.

Crisp air and rosy cheeks to gain,
On your heart it will make an indelible stain.

The experience will recompense itself.

When the stars begin to burn you will sense it.

www.ingramcontent.com/pod-product-compliance
Lightning Source LLC
LaVergne TN
LVHW051239200726

843510LV00011B/1617